Fundamental
KARATE

Instructor Larry Brusacoram and the following athletes were photographed for this book:
Chris Balus,
Jenny Cook,
Jerry Nguyen,
Katherine Trang Nguyen,
Amber Watroba,
R. J. Wilbur, and
Paul Yerich.

Fundamental
KARATE

Kim Dallas

Photographs by Andy King

Lerner Publications Company
Minneapolis

Without the long-standing support of my husband, Andrew, and my three wonderful children, this book would not have been possible. I am indebted to them for their patience and understanding as I pursue my dreams.

My deepest thanks to my first karate instructors, Mike Kotasek and Katie Morris, for their knowledge and support. Without them, I would've never discovered both the joy and agony of this beautiful sport.

Website address: www.lernerbooks.com

The Fundamental Sports series was conceptualized by editor Julie Jensen, designed by graphic artist Michael Tacheny, and composed on a Macintosh computer by Robert Mauzy. The Fundamental Sports series was designed in conjunction with the Beginning Sports series to offer young athletes a basic understanding of various sports at two reading levels.

Photo Acknowledgments
Photographs are reproduced with the permission of: pp. 7, 8, © Dennis Cox/China Stock; p. 9, © ALL-SPORT USA/Doug Pensinger; p. 44, Courtesy of Jhoon Rhee, Fountain of Youth Foundation.

Library of Congress Cataloging-in-Publication Data

Dallas, Kim.
   Fundamental karate / Kim Dallas ; photographs by Andy King.
     p. cm.—(Fundamental sports)
   Includes bibliographical references and index.
   Summary: An introduction to the history, skills, and techniques of karate.
   ISBN 0-8225-3462-2 (alk. paper)
   1. Karate—Juvenile literature. [1. Karate.] I. King, Andy, ill. II. Title. III. Series.
GV1114.3.D35 1998
796.815'3—dc21   97-29623

Manufactured in the United States of America
1 2 3 4 5 6 – JR – 03 02 01 00 99 98

Contents

Chapter 1

How This Sport Got Started

Martial arts moves can be as graceful as a ballet dancer's, yet as explosive as a boxer's. Martial artists can use so much strength and energy during a two-minute routine that they finish the exercise exhausted. Jumping, kicking, punching, and blocking are all part of a student's training. Martial arts moves are designed to help them become physically fit and to help them protect themselves if they are attacked.

The practice of martial arts began in Asia. Karate is one of many martial art forms. Other martial arts include tae kwon do, aikido, judo, and kung fu. These various styles originated in Japan, China, Thailand, India, and Korea. In early Asian history, members of royalty were the only people who had weapons such as knives and swords. Common people had to learn fighting techniques to defend themselves. These techniques depended on the individual's terrain and lifestyle.

Murals and other artwork from ancient times show us how early athletes practiced and performed their martial arts. This mural is in the People's Republic of China.

7

Hundreds of years ago, Buddhist monks recognized the benefits of physical activity on mental and spiritual development. These statues of monks are in the Shaolin Temple in China.

Southern Chinese fighters, for example, developed a fighting style that used low stances because they needed to keep their balance on muddy ground or on boats. Northern Chinese fighters lived in mountainous regions. Their fighting style used a more upright stance to deliver powerful kicks to attackers on horses. Okinawan farmers used their farming tools to defend themselves. Koreans added spinning kicks to enhance their style.

Karate, which means "empty hand," began in Japan. Gichin Funakoshi (foo-nah-KO-shee) is known as the father of modern karate. He established systems of learning karate moves throughout Japan.

Americans learned about karate during World War II and the Korean War. U.S. soldiers saw people using these fighting styles. The Americans were impressed and they wanted to learn how to fight that way. Ed Parker and Robert Trias were early American martial artists who opened schools and trained students.

Many styles of karate were brought to the United States, and many karate schools have combined traditional styles with more modern moves. Despite the adjustments, some universal principles haven't changed. All forms of karate require respect, control, discipline, and practice.

Karate once was used only to cause harm to an attacker. Now, in **sport karate**, a karate student can practice and have fun doing moves against an actual opponent without trying to hurt him or her. Sport karate tournaments are held all over the country and include all levels of competitors, from beginning to advanced. Competitions are offered in **sparring** (fighting) or **kata** (routines) events.

The Many Faces of Martial Arts

Here are some of the most popular styles of martial arts:

Tae Kwon Do

Tae kwon do is a Korean-based martial art that emphasizes kicks and punches. One of its trademarks is the powerful side kick. Although tae kwon do has been around since the first century, Korea did not formally recognize it as a martial arts style until 1955. Jhoon Rhee brought this style to the United States in the 1960s. Tae kwon do is the most popular style taught in martial arts schools.

Kung fu

Kung fu is the term Americans use to refer to Chinese martial arts. Many of these moves rely on foot and hand techniques that are rooted in nature. Monks in the sixth century carefully studied animals to learn how they hunted. Then, the monks imitated the animals' movements. In this art form, styles such as the praying mantis, white crane, tiger, and monkey are often used against opponents. Just as with many styles of martial arts, perfecting these moves, which are spectacular displays of balance and strength, can take years.

Judo

Judo is a Japanese martial art that focuses on throwing and grappling techniques. Jigaro Kano founded the style in 1882 after years of studying jujitsu, another type of martial art. He focused on immobilizing attackers by using their own momentum against them.

In a competition, such as the Olympics, contestants are awarded points for throwing an opponent by using good technique, putting an opponent on his or her back, applying an immobilizing hold for 30 seconds, or performing combination moves. Students practice on soft mats where they can be thrown to the floor without injuring themselves or their fellow students.

Aikido

Some say Aikido is one of the most sophisticated martial arts. Morihei Uyeshiba found that by moving opponents into a circular

motion, he could then place their limbs into a joint lock. Uyeshiba used his opponents' own momentum against them. He was surprised to find that doing so did not require much physical strength and was a very successful way to defend himself. In 1926, he opened a school in Tokyo, Japan, and began training students in this highly effective technique.

His idea caught on and many students have learned this impressive style, which wasn't designed to cause serious injury but to gain control over an attacker. Many American police departments have found this style to be very useful in training their officers.

Chapter 2

BASICS

Karate includes mental as well as physical challenges. Finding a school (called a *dojo* in Japan) with a positive learning atmosphere is an important first step for any karate student.

Schools emphasize different aspects of karate. Some focus on self-defense techniques. Others teach traditional martial arts. Some schools have changed traditional movements to make karate more a sport than a martial art.

Your age and interests will help you determine which type of school is best for you. For instance, if you are six years old, you may want to go to a school that emphasizes discipline and building self-confidence. If you are 16 years old, you may feel that self-defense is important. You might pick a school that gives you more sparring classes. Whatever school you choose, you should be comfortable with the instructor and the facility because karate training can be intense.

The Beginning—the Bow

*Bowing may not seem like such a big deal, or even look that difficult, but a properly executed **bow** is important. Above, Amber demonstrates a correct bow. She stands with her fingers closed, palms open, and arms close to her sides. Her toes and heels are touching each other. She looks directly in front of herself throughout the bow. Students typically begin class by bowing to their instructor as a group. When all the students are ready, they all bend at the waist and bow together. Amber's hands and arms should stay perfectly still along her pants legs as she completes the move.*

11

Karate is usually practiced in a large room with mirrors covering one wall so the students can see themselves and their instructor demonstrate different moves. The floor is often highly polished wood or wood covered with a thin layer of carpeting to ensure proper footing and balance. Sometimes a bar is positioned along one wall for students to use when stretching out or practicing difficult moves.

Before and after each class, students line up in front of their instructor, become silent, and bow. This is a sign of respect between the students and the instructor. Bowing also shows that the students trust the instructor to teach them the basics of discipline, respect, and fundamentals. All three of these basics are important in martial arts.

Warmup

Early in their training, karate students learn the importance of stretching out their entire body before starting to practice maneuvers. Stretching not only prevents injury to tendons and muscles, it helps students become more flexible in all their moves. Flexibility is important in karate training.

Often, the highest ranking student leads the class in the stretching exercises. Students are especially careful to stretch out the hips and groin area. Many karate moves use these body parts, and these areas can easily be injured.

Students begin their stretching routine by gently bending their heads in all directions. This helps stretch their neck muscles.

Next, students extend one leg for-ward while pushing their weight onto their front legs and keeping their back legs straight and on the floor. This stretches the quadriceps muscles on the tops of their thighs. By straightening out the front leg and bending over at the waist, the students next stretch the hamstring muscles in the back of their legs.

Next, students spread their legs apart about two shoulder widths and bend at the waist, forming a triangle. This helps stretch hamstring and groin muscles. Students then sit on the floor with their legs extended and try to touch their chins to their knees. This further stretches hamstring muscles.

By bringing their feet together, forming a "butterfly" position, the students stretch their groin and hip muscles.

They stretch their shoulders by crossing one arm across their body and gently pressing with the opposite arm.

After the individual stretches are finished, students use a partner to help them stretch their limbs even further with some resistance. This helps them become even more flexible.

Some students might say that stretching out is boring. When you consider that preventing a muscle pull only takes a few minutes of stretching, but rehabilitating that muscle after a serious injury can take months, stretching seems worthwhile.

The Yell

One of the very first things a karate student learns is how and when to yell during a karate move. Does it seem ridiculous to have to learn to yell? After all, most of us have been yelling for our whole lives. A karate yell is different from a regular yell in several ways.

A karate yell is abrupt and powerful, not high-pitched or whiny. A karate student's yell is designed to make an attacker think twice about harming you. Although everyone's yell is distinctive, the most effective yells come from deep within the lungs and windpipe. If you contract your stomach muscles at the exact moment you yell, you will produce a more commanding sound.

Another important reason karate students yell is to ready themselves for defense. The first fighting position in karate is always accompanied by a yell. Even after months of training, a karate student recognizes the yell as part of being ready.

Yelling is also an important part of breathing during karate. Sometimes students hold their breath when they are sparring or defending themselves. They are concentrating on their actions and they forget to breathe. Yelling helps them breath properly.

Equipment

A karate student wears a loose-fitting top and pants called a **gi** *(gee)*. A gi is usually made of cotton, which is light-weight and comfortable so students can do their moves with the greatest amount of flexibility. The uniforms come in a variety of colors and often have patches or insignias displaying

Some of the different colors of karate belts are shown below. Students try to move up to a higher belt level, as indicated by the color of the belt. To do so, they must pass tests given by their instructors. Some students wear lightweight karate shoes, shown in the bottom photo, but many students prefer to go barefoot.

the school's name and the student's name. Most students buy their gi from the karate school they attend or a martial arts supply store.

Students wear cotton belts around their waists, tied in a square knot, to indicate their skill level. In most schools, white, gold, or yellow belts are given to beginning students. The intermediate students wear belts of green, blue, or purple. Red or brown belts indicate advanced students. In order for a student to receive a new belt, he or she must pass a belt test. Students who have mastered a number of requirements set by the school are allowed to wear a black belt.

Most karate students train in bare feet for balance and control. Some students choose to wear karate shoes. Karate shoes are made of very soft leather with thin flat rubber soles.

Typical Class

After the bow, the karate instructor will call out a "Ready" command. This signals the students to take a formal position in order to receive their next instruction. Schools use different ready positions. The ready position shown in the photograph to the right is called chunbi. Jenny's feet are shoulder width apart, with her fists clenched at belt level.

Often, the instructor focuses the day's lesson on one type of move. The instructor will call out different commands for practice moves. For instance, if the focus of the lesson is hand techniques, the instructor may have students practice several different hand movements. For each move, the instructor helps the students get their feet, hands, and body into the correct position.

The lesson may also include practicing with partners, or in front of the mirror, or with pads in order to develop the correct technique. In some schools, the instructors have the students play karate games. Card games, relay races, and Simon Says are favorites of many students.

Classes can be as small as one student and as big as 20. An even number of students is ideal because then it's easy to find partners for drills. A class shouldn't be so big that students don't have enough room to do moves without hitting other students.

Taking a class is the best way to learn karate. That way, you will have a safe area in which to practice.

Chapter 3

THE MOVES

Karate moves can be classified into two types—classical and practical. Classical moves are rooted firmly in traditional martial arts styles. Practical moves are adaptations of classical moves for self-defense situations. Classical martial arts moves can take a lifetime to perfect, but many students learn the practical styles quickly and can effectively use them when needed.

On the following pages, you will see karate students demonstrating various moves. You can learn a lot from looking at their form, but the best way for you to learn karate is by taking a class. The instructor and other students will help you do the moves correctly and safely.

Most karate moves are based on body position and use the entire body. For instance, a **punch** is not delivered with just the arms and shoulders. A student must use his or her hips and legs to drive the fist into the target for a strong karate punch. Also, when a student understands angles and the way a person's joints, such as elbows and knees, bend, the student can handle a seemingly stronger opponent.

In a classical move, the student's feet stay flat on the floor, as in the photograph above. In a practical move, the student's heel may leave the floor, as demonstrated in the photo below.

19

Fighting Stance

One of the first moves a karate student learns is a correct **stance**. The stance prepares the student for any move.

In a practical fighting stance at left, Paul stands sideways to his attacker. His front hand is raised in a tight fist to protect his face. His other hand is held close to his body, also in a tight fist. Notice how his knees are slightly bent and his legs are comfortably apart. Paul is careful to focus on his target and is ready to defend himself.

Hand Strikes

Hand strikes are usually the easiest techniques that the beginning karate student learns. Some hand strikes are quick, like the **backfist** and the **jab**. Others are powerful, like the punch, **hammerfist**, and **palm heel**. All hand strikes require careful positioning and practice.

● *Punch*

The punch is one of the first hand techniques karate students learn. The student begins by holding the punching hand close to the body in a tightly closed fist with the palm turned up. The thumb is curled across the fingers on the outside. Some beginners tuck their thumb inside their fingers. This is dangerous because they could break their own thumb when they hit the pad or the opponent.

In the top two photos on the next page, Chris shows how a practical punch is delivered. He starts in a practical stance. Then Chris raises his heel

off the ground and drives his hips and his arm forward for the most power. As he extends his arm, he rotates his fist and finishes with the palm facing down.

From a classical stance, at right, R. J. moves his front foot over for better balance and then throws the punch with both feet flat on the ground. R. J. and Chris both keep their backs straight to avoid losing their balance and falling into their target. R. J. and Chris strike the target with their first two large knuckles into either the chest or the face of an attacker.

● *Jab*

The jab is a quick-striking weapon that is best when delivered to an attacker's face. Katherine starts off in a fighting stance with her fists tightly closed as if she's going to punch. Her feet are set comfortably apart with her weight centered over her body.

With her front hand, Katherine shoots out her arm in a straight thrusting motion. Notice how Katherine lunges forward and shifts her weight toward her attacker. She strikes the opponent's face with her two largest knuckles.

● *Hammerfist*

To throw a hammerfist, Jerry starts in the same fighting stance as he would to throw a punch. But, instead of thrusting his rear fist forward, Jerry reaches up behind and above his head. Then he strikes down on his opponent's nose with the bottom of his fist.

Jerry's hips and feet are in the same position as if he had delivered a punch. His front hand hardly moves, keeping his face protected throughout the move.

● *Palm Heel*

The palm heel is another effective hand technique. Jenny starts off as if she's ready to punch, but the palm of her striking hand is open. For her palm heel to be effective, Jenny curls her fingers tightly and presses her thumb against her hand.

For a practical palm heel, Jenny drives her hips forward and raises her heel in the same way that she would if she had thrown a punch. At the moment of impact, her wrist is cocked back. The blow lands right below the attacker's nose.

In a classical palm heel, Jenny would keep her feet flat on the ground in a wide stance. Either way, after the hit,

Jenny can open up her fingers and rake them across the opponent's face, further disabling the attacker.

Kicks

A variety of powerful kicks are used in karate. Some kicks are better used for self-defense. Others are used mainly in competitions.

To be effective kickers, karate students must have power, flexibility, correct positioning, and speed. The smaller person often uses kicks against a larger attacker because a person's reach and power are much greater with kicks than with hand strikes.

● *Round Kick*

A **round kick** is a fast and powerful kick. Round kicks are generally used offensively, or when a person is initiating contact, because they are so quick.

Jenny shows how to throw a round kick correctly in the photographs at right. She first rolls over her hip and then pulls her knee waist high, back and slightly wide of her opponent. Jenny then snaps out her leg and strikes the opponent with the top side of her foot. She keeps her hands close to her body for protection. Immediately after contact, Jenny snaps her leg back and out of the way of an attacker.

The best target areas for a round kick are the head, stomach, and chest. In sport karate, round kicks are used to score quick points in sparring. Round kicks are not often used in self-defense because they do not generate enough power to disable an opponent.

● *Side Kick*

A **side kick** is one of the strongest kicks in karate. When delivered properly, a side kick can bring an attacker to an immediate halt. Side kicks are important weapons for any karate student. Depending on how flexible the karate student is, he or she may aim for the attacker's chest or neck.

From a fighting stance, Chris first brings his leg in tight toward his body and rolls over his hip. This sets him up to explosively extend his leg into the target. At the moment of impact, he locks his knee. His other leg leans forward into the attacker for even greater power. After snapping out his leg, Chris tightly coils his leg back to his body so the attacker cannot grab it.

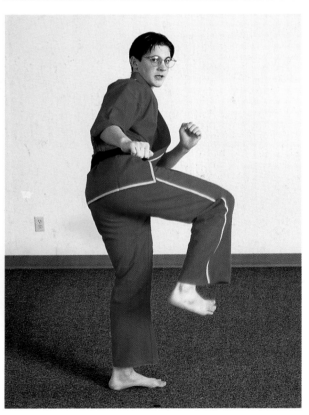

● *Side Stomp*

A slight variation of the side kick is the **side stomp**, which can be used on the knee or ankle of an attacker. Amber demonstrates a correct side stomp.

Notice how Amber pulls her knee back completely to her waist before she strikes. Amber locks her knee in place as she strikes the target with her heel. Many students pretend they are stomping on pop cans to practice the correct technique.

● *Front Kick*

The **front kick** is another powerful kick karate students use to hit an attacker's head, chest, or groin. Often, students will use a front kick defensively. From a fighting stance, R. J. first lifts his front knee straight up and waist high. His foot points down, but his toes are curled backward. He will strike his target with the ball of his foot so that he won't break his toes on contact. R. J. keeps his hands and arms up during the entire kick. After he hits the target, he quickly snaps his foot back.

● *Thrust Kick*

The thrust kick is a variation of the front kick. A thrust kick starts like a front kick as the student first pulls her knee into her chest. Then, as Katherine demonstrates, instead of snapping out the kick, she thrusts her weight completely forward and into the target as the kick is delivered. Thrust kicks are usually used offensively.

Blocks

Because karate is based on self-defense, knowing how to block an attacker's strikes is very important. The **high block, forearm block,** and **low block** are the most common self-defense blocks. In all of these blocks, students use the forearm as the blocking tool because of its large surface area. Students learn the proper timing and technique, as well as improve their reaction time, by practicing these blocks over and over.

● High Block

The high block is a very effective block for attacks to the head and face. Jerry demonstrates this block in the photos at right. First, he crosses his forearms in front of his body. Then, he snaps his top arm over his head. Jerry is careful not to have his blocking arm in front of his face or directly on top of his head. If he did, someone could slam his blocking arm back into his body. Jerry's non-blocking hand is pulled in tight to his chest, ready to strike. Jerry stands in a fighting stance, slightly bending his knees for support and balance during the block.

● *Forearm Block*

The forearm block helps a student defend against strikes to the chest and face. Amber illustrates the correct stance for an outside forearm block. She starts in a fighting stance, then crosses her arms in front of her. She then thrusts her forearm out and away from her body to block the oncoming strike. Notice how her blocking arm stays bent throughout the block. Her non-blocking hand stays close to her body to protect herself or throw a punch.

● *Low Block*

Students use the low block primarily against kicking attacks to the groin and stomach. To do a low block, Paul first raises his blocking hand, with the palm turned in, up by his ear and keeps his arm close to his body. Then Paul snaps out his fist toward the kick, rotating his palm down, and, at the same time, shifts his front foot for balance. He then bends his front knee, which forces his weight forward.

Chapter 4

SELF-DEFENSE

Karate is based on the idea that it is better to avoid a fight than to get into one. All karate practitioners, even black belts, are honored for knowing how to walk away from fighting as well as for how to disable someone. If someone is threatening you, first try talking with him or her or with your teachers or parents. If nothing else stops the threatening person, your last option is self-defense.

No one has the right to injure you. You have the right to protect yourself. When you have a clear idea of some self-defense strategies, you will be in a better position to survive an attack.

There are many different ways an attacker can come at you and there are just as many different ways to defend yourself. All karate schools have their own styles. There isn't any one "right" way to protect yourself. However, the key to any of these moves is to practice them over and over again so your self-defense reflexes become automatic if you ever need them. Here are a few common grabs and escape ideas.

Training Aids

Many students use training aids to help them develop power and focus. Heavy body shields, or pads, are used to help a student develop powerful kicks. A partner holds the pad while the student visualizes an attacker. When the instructor gives the command, the student steps forward slightly and kicks explosively into the pad. The padding allows the student to kick as hard as he or she can without hurting the partner.

Smaller hand pads are also effective training devices. These are often used for punching and kicking combinations. For example, the instructor may set up the students with partners and then yell "Jab, punch, round kick!" Often the instructor will have students do the drill with both their right and left hands or feet so that both sides of their body get a workout.

Some schools use old X-ray papers for students to practice their aim. Above, Katherine works on keeping her knee level while doing a round kick. She's more concerned that her technique is correct and directed at the right place on the paper than she is about the force delivered.

Choke Hold

A choke hold is a frightening move. However, think fast and you can go on the offensive. Realize that both your arms and legs are free and your opponent's wrists are the weak link.

Katherine demonstrates how to get out of a choke hold. She grabs her opponent's arm with her left hand and reaches back with her right fist. She quickly twists her body while striking through both wrists of her attacker to break the hold.

After breaking the hold, Katherine could pull her knee to her waist and thrust a side stomp to her attacker's knee. Other methods would work, too. For example, Katherine could quickly strike her attacker with a knee to the groin or a palm heel to the face.

Wrist Grab

If you simply pull back from a wrist grab, the attacker will undoubtedly squeeze tighter. The key to escaping wrist grabs is twisting through the weakest link—the thumb. One simple way to do this is to pull up and through the attacker's thumb and index finger. If you are uncomfortable doing this, you can also disable your attacker without escaping.

In the example shown, Paul grabs Jerry's wrist. Jerry quickly raises his knee to his waist and stomps down at Paul's knee. If Paul continues to hold on, Jerry steps forward and throws a hammerfist to Paul's face.

Shoulder Grab

If an attacker grabs your shoulder or the front of your shirt, remember you have an advantage because both your arms and legs are free. Chris demonstrates how to escape quickly. He steps back with the foot opposite the shoulder that is being grabbed. Chris then throws a high block as close to the attacker's wrist as possible. In the photos, R.J. grabs Chris' left shoulder, so Chris steps back with his right leg.

This move puts Chris in an ideal position to follow the escape with a front kick to the groin. Chris twists his body to get the most power at the point of impact. Chris would complete the move by grabbing the attacker's shoulder and throwing his knees into R.J.'s groin.

Grab from Behind

Calm and quick thinking can put you on the offensive, even in this scary and dangerous position, when someone grabs you from behind. Amber demonstrates. She immediately raises her left arm and steps behind and toward her attacker with her left leg. She then twists her body to break the hold and throws a palm heel into the attacker's face.

Bear Hug

Katherine demonstrates one quick and easy method to get away from a bear hug. Katherine side stomps her attacker's ankle, which forces him to loosen his grip. She then steps to one side of the attacker and strikes his groin with a hammerfist. Afterward, she quickly gets back into a fighting stance.

Hammerlock

If the attacker has cranked back your right arm and grabbed your left shoulder, you are in a hammerlock. In the photos at right, Jenny demonstrates one way to get out of this situation.

First, she steps back with her left leg, as if she's walking toward her attacker. Then, she lifts her left arm and points her elbow straight out in front of her. Next, Jenny twists around quickly and drops her left arm across the attacker's body, pinning down her arm. This breaks the hold and sets up Jenny to strike the attacker's face with her elbow. To do this, Jenny pulls back her left arm and then thrusts it forward toward the attacker's jaw.

Keep in mind that the best strikes to use if you are attacked from the front are the punch, palm heel, hammerfist, front kick, knee to groin, and side stomp. The best strikes to try if you are attacked from behind are the hammerfist, grab to the groin, elbow to the body or face, and side stomp.

Don't try these moves until you have learned them from a qualified instructor and practiced them. These moves can be dangerous and should only be practiced with supervision and proper equipment. And always remember, avoiding a fight is better than winning one.

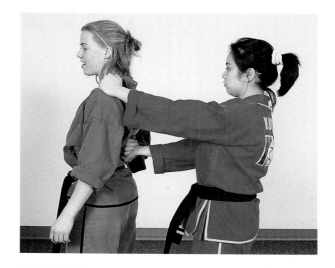

Chapter 5

COMPETITION

Sport karate tournaments give students a chance to test their skills against opponents from other schools. Once a student steps into a tournament ring, he or she faces an opponent about whom they know very little. They must perform despite their anxiety. This anxiety is somewhat similar to what a person might experience if he or she was attacked. After all, if you are ever in a threatening situation, you probably will feel anxious and afraid. Some instructors feel that dealing with this fear is a crucial part of training. Fear and adrenaline can cause athletes to forget what they've learned. Tournaments can be a safe place to simulate that fear and test one's abilities.

The major divisions of a tournament are the kata and sparring. Students are divided by belt rank, and sometimes by age, size, and sex so that the competition is equal and fair. Usually, boys and girls who are younger than 11 compete together because body size is the most important factor. For example, a small boy blue belt may be matched against a small girl blue belt. Girls and boys older than 11 participate in separate

This karate student is competing in the weapons kata division. Weapons used in competition are not sharpened.

Jhoon Rhee

In the early 1960s, Jhoon Rhee excited audiences with his spectacular board-breaking techniques, which he demonstrated in American colleges. Many students were so impressed by his style that they wanted his instruction. As his popularity grew, so did his list of interested students. Soon, Rhee became well-known around the country as the master of tae kwon do. Members of the Secret Service and Pentagon, and other government officials trained under his leadership. Even movie star martial artist Bruce Lee learned how to do a stunning side kick from Rhee.

As his style of training spread nationwide, other schools wanted to adapt many of his methods. The Jhoon Rhee System focuses on natural body positions that enhance power and speed during a move. It also incorporates many different forms of martial arts. Like other martial art styles, the Jhoon Rhee System teaches discipline, respect, and control.

divisions. All students regardless of age, sex, or belt are required to compete at the highest belt level they have achieved. Local, state, regional, national, and international tournaments are held all over the world.

At the registration desk, students decide the areas in which they want to compete. Their school, age, rank, and size are all recorded. After the student pays an entry fee, he or she is assigned a ring number and event time. Many students arrive early to watch and study other opponents in hopes of calming their fears before it's their turn to enter the ring.

Kata

Many students enjoy performing a kata, or a sequence of karate moves. Katas give a student the opportunity to demonstrate speed, skill, intensity, and precision in executing karate moves. A kata, or form, is not a series of moves randomly put together. Much like the routine of a gymnast or ballet dancer, a kata has specific moves that must be done accurately. The student is judged according to how well he or she performs the moves.

Beginning karate students start with katas that are designed for newcomers to the sport. A beginner's kata may involve only punching, blocking, and two changes of direction. Advanced students perform katas that include jumps, spins, punches, blocks, and as many as eight changes of direction.

A student might choose to do a certain kata to reflect his or her own strengths. For instance, some katas focus on power and others showcase speed and flexibility. Traditional katas are as old as the sport itself. Others were developed by high-ranking black belt masters in American schools. Some schools even allow black belt students to make up their own katas.

Katas can be divided into several types, which represent specialties of the major karate schools. Students often compete in more than one category.

● *Musical*

Musical katas are particularly interesting for spectators to watch. The karate moves are timed to match the music, much like a gymnast's floor routine.

● *Asian*

Asian katas reflect the traditional forms. In some schools, only Asian katas are performed. These katas are not performed to music and do not include any elements of gymnastics or other non-traditional techniques.

● *Weapons*

In the weapons division, competitors use the **bo**, machete-like knives, and the three-pronged **sai**. The students whip their weapons around with such power and precision that a spectator can actually hear the air whoosh by and almost see the object the student is

In the photos below and on the next two pages, Amber does some of the moves in a beginner's kata.

pretending to stab. To prevent injuries, students don't use sharp weapons.

● *American*

In this category, students can show off the many different katas their schools have developed. Some students combine gymnastics moves, such as flips and jumps, with karate moves. Some traditional martial arts instructors frown on this type of kata because it goes against tradition. However, the American kata divisions are very popular and many schools teach this style.

● *Judging*

To begin a kata competition, the student steps into the ring and announces his or her name, school, and kata. This can be a nerve-wracking time for the students. Even though they have practiced their routine hundreds of times, they may for-

Traditional katas were developed by the ancient masters to instruct and to test students.

get their own name during the introduction! Luckily, judges do not lower scores if that happens.

After bowing to the judges, the student performs the kata. Experienced black belts judge the competitors in every kata division. They judge the student on accuracy of the moves, fluidity of the routine, and his or her intensity. Katas were developed to simulate imaginary fights with fierce opponents, and judges want the student to perform the moves so convincingly that the judge can almost see the student's attacker in the ring.

The judges decide on a score from a low 7.0 to the highest score of 10.0 points. Hundredth intervals allow judges to be precise in scoring. After all competitors have performed, the judges announce the first, second, and third place winners.

Amber does punches and blocks as part of her kata. Jumps and kicks are included in other katas.

Katherine's smile shows off her clear mouth-guard. In addition to a mouthguard, students wear protective padding on their heads, hands, and midsections when they spar.

Sparring

Sparring is a competition in which karate students put all their moves together against an actual opponent. Many students think this is the most fun way to use their karate skills. They are eager to move beyond beginner status so they can spar.

Any fighting, whether practice or real, can be dangerous and that is why most schools only allow students who have mastered some basic principles of karate to participate. Practice fighting helps students develop quick reflexes, and build up their endurance and confidence in a safe setting. Everyone wears protective gear while sparring to prevent injuries.

In some karate schools, sparring is divided into drills and free sparring. Instructors teach students timing, defensive techniques, and strategies, such as setting up a hand or foot strike. Then the students usually spend a part of each class actually fighting for two to three minutes under the instructor's supervision. The free sparring sessions are short, but they can be exhausting for the beginning student. Most beginners feel an adrenaline rush when someone first attacks them. Beginners often either throw wild punches or tense up and do nothing. Both of these approaches wear down a new student. However, as students learn more about fighting, they start to understand how to relax during a fight. They begin to be able to conserve their energy and throw only the most efficient moves. These skills are especially important in competitions.

Another goal for students during

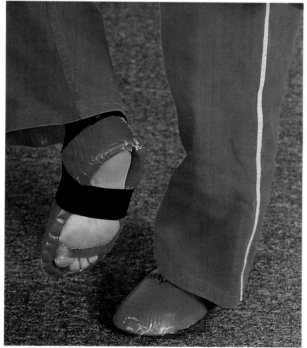

Above, Jenny and Katherine practice their moves during a sparring session. At left, students wear protective pads on their feet while sparring.

sparring class is to learn how to avoid being hit. This sounds easier than it is. Experienced karate fighters are experts at setting up moves so their opponent doesn't see what's coming. Some people have compared sparring matches to chess. When they spar, karate students must match not only their power and speed but also their wits against an opponent.

● *Point Sparring*

Point sparring allows students to test their strength against students from other schools. The center judge (a black belt) or the timekeeper calls the two contestants into a ring. The students stand opposite each other and bow. The center judge holds his or her hand between the two contestants. To start the two-minute match, the center judge raises his or her arm while saying, "Fight."

Judges score a sparring event differently than they do a kata competition. As strikes are thrown in a sparring match, three judges will decide if a point was awarded. Two out of the

three judges have to agree that a clean strike hit a legal target area with controlled contact before awarding a point.

Fighters must remember that the goal is to score the most points, up to five, in a two-minute period, not to hurt the other student. Different belt levels may have special scoring rules, depending on the tournament. In most cases, punches thrown to the body or head are worth one point and kicks thrown are worth two points. Each punch or kick must strike the target

area clearly and without interference from another part of the body. Legal target areas include the head, face, chest, ribs, abdomen, and kidneys. The groin, knees, ankles, back, and neck are illegal target areas.

In the photos at left, R. J. and Chris demonstrate some punches, blocks, and kicks that might be used in a match.

If a student did an illegal move during the match, the judges would warn him or her. If the student did a second illegal move, the judges would give the opponent a point. If the student did an illegal move a third time, he or she would be disqualified.

RAZZLE DAZZLE

Karate movies and popular television shows have sent many students to karate schools, seeking to learn some of the incredible moves they saw their favorite hero perform. Remember, camera angles, lights, and special effects can all make a karate move look spectacular. A real karate master, however, doesn't need any of those aids to impress an audience.

Black belt students practice for years to develop incredible speed and flexibility for their moves. In the photo on this page, Jerry shows off a jump spin wheel kick. This move requires awesome spinning speed and control. In order to achieve this, Jerry spent hours breaking down the move. First, he jumped and spun without the kick. Then, as his body became stronger, he worked on adding the kick. Then, he spent hours practicing in front of the mirror to develop a balanced spin and kick.

Exhibition moves are fun to watch at karate tournaments also. Below, Jerry, Chris, and Jenny work together for a perfectly timed jump split kick.

Spectators love to see karate masters break boards. Many black belts enjoy combining height, spins, and speed when board-breaking. Some prefer to side kick a board. Others like to punch the board and others use an elbow strike, as Paul does above.

To break this board, Paul first directs his partner to hold the board at the exact height he needs. Paul focuses on his target and lines up his elbow and feet, slowly rehearsing the move. When Paul is ready, he shifts his weight forward and thrusts his elbow through the board, giving a loud yell at impact.

Any karate master needs to be flexible. In the photo above, Jenny demonstrates her flexibility. Notice how straight up and down her legs are. Jenny has paid careful attention to stretching before her workouts to achieve this amount of flexibility. At left, Chris illustrates how he uses his flexibility in an impressive side kick.

Tornado kicks are exciting to watch. They can also be effective weapons once perfected. R. J. performs his tornado kick with accurate balance and control. He spins around 360 degrees and keeps his body almost straight up and down at the time of the kick.

All karate moves require lots of practice. Still, the rewards of studying karate go far beyond performing dynamite kicks or facing up to bullies. Karate is a fun and exciting sport for any athlete who chooses to develop physical prowess and mental toughness.

KARATE TALK

backfist: A punch thrown by swinging the forearm away from the body with the palm facing inward. The target is hit with the back of the fist.

bo: A long, rounded wooden stick used in a weapons kata.

bow: A move done by bending forward at the waist. A bow is a traditional sign of respect between students and instructor, and between sparring partners.

forearm block: A defensive move in which the karate student sweeps a forearm in front of his or her body to block attacks to the chest or face.

front kick: A defensive move in which the karate student extends a leg directly in front of him- or herself. The student uses the ball of the foot to strike an opponent.

gi: The standard karate uniform of a loose-fitting top and wide-legged pants. The uniform is closed with a belt, the color of which indicates the student's ability.

hammerfist: A strike performed with a tightly closed fist used with a powerful sweeping motion.

high block: A defensive move in which the karate student uses a forearm raised above the head to block attacks to the face and head.

Paul, Jenny, and Jerry are each using a bo in this weapons kata.

jab: A quick, tight-fisted punch that is delivered straight on.

kata: A series of traditional martial arts moves that are done in a specific sequence or routine.

low block: A defensive move in which the karate student uses a forearm to block attacks to the groin and stomach.

outside block: A defensive move in which the karate student uses a forearm to push away any attacks to the chest or face.

palm heel: A punch that is delivered with the fingers curled tightly down and the palm facing outward to strike the target.

punch: A strike that is delivered with a tight fist. The hand is held close to the body before the student strikes the target with the two largest knuckles first.

round kick: A fast kick in which the karate student uses a snapping motion and strikes the target with the top of the foot.

sai: A three-pronged weapon that is used in a weapons kata.

side kick: A powerful kick in which the karate student extends a locked leg and strikes an opponent in his or her chest or face with the heel of the extended leg.

side stomp: A move in which the karate student extends a leg sideward and downward to strike an opponent's knee or ankle.

sparring: A form of controlled fighting in which two karate students wearing protective gear use punches, kicks, jabs, and blocks to strike each other. Competitive sparring is done on a 26-foot square mat.

sport karate: A form of competitive karate in which karate students use their moves against actual opponents without harming them.

stance: A position the karate student takes before beginning a move.

Chris, R. J., and Katherine demonstrate side kicks of various heights.

FURTHER READING

Blot, Pierre. *Karate for Beginners*. New York: Sterling, 1996.

Corcoran, John. *The Martial Arts Sourcebook*. New York: Harper Perennial, 1994.

Goedecke, Christopher. *Smart Moves*. New York: Simon and Schuster, 1995.

Metil, Luana and Jace Townsend. *The Story of Karate*. Minneapolis: Lerner Publications, 1995.

Mitchell, David. *The Young Martial Arts Enthusiast*. New York: DK Publishing, Inc., 1997.

Morris, Ann. *Karate Boy*. New York: Dutton, 1996.

Queen, J. Allen. *Complete Karate*. New York: Sterling, 1993.

Queen, J. Allen. *Karate Basics*. Minneapolis: Lerner Publications, 1992.

FOR MORE INFORMATION

Aikido Association of America
1016 W. Belmont
Chicago, IL 60657

All American Taekwon-do Federation
P. O. Box 9430
Wilmington, DE 19809

American Ju-Jitsu Association
P. O. Box 1357
Burbank, CA 91507

American Karate Association
P. O. Box 214
Momence, IL 60954

American Karate Federation
250 New Litchfield St.
Torrington, CT 06790

American Kenpo Karate Association
6469 S. W. 8th St.
Miami, FL 33144

American Taekwon-do Association
6210 Baseline Road
Little Rock, AR 72209

International Ninja Society
P. O. Box 1221
Dublin, OH 43017

National Women's Martial Arts
   Federation
5680 San Pablo Ave.
Oakland, CA 94608

North American Amateur Contact
   Karate/Kickboxing Association
255 S. W. Higgins
Missoula, MT 59803

United States Judo Federation
19 North Union Blvd.
Colorado Springs, CO 80909

United States Karate Association
P. O. Box 17135
Phoenix, AZ 85011

United States Taekwondo Association
220 E. 86th St.
New York, NY 10028

INDEX

10/98